THE ZEN of STEVE JOBS

WRITTEN BY CALEB MELBY

OF **Forbes**

CONCEPT, DESIGN, AND ILLUSTRATION BY JESS3

WILEY

JOHN WILEY & SONS, INC.

THE ZEN of STEVE JOBS

PUBLISHED BY JOHN WILEY & SONS, INC., HOBOKEN, NEW JERSEY.

PUBLISHED SIMULTANEOUSLY IN CANADA.

FOR GENERAL INFORMATION ON OUR OTHER PRODUCTS AND SERVICES OR
FOR TECHNICAL SUPPORT, PLEASE CONTACT OUR CUSTOMER CARE DE-
PARTMENT WITHIN THE UNITED STATES AT (800) 762-2974, OUTSIDE
THE UNITED STATES AT (317) 572-3993 OR FAX (317) 572-4002.

WILEY ALSO PUBLISHES ITS BOOKS IN A VARIETY OF ELECTRONIC FORMATS.
SOME CONTENT THAT APPEARS IN PRINT MAY NOT BE AVAILABLE IN ELEC-
TRONIC BOOKS. FOR MORE INFORMATION ABOUT WILEY PRODUCTS, VISIT
OUR WEB SITE AT WWW.WILEY.COM.

ISBN 978-1-118-29526-7; ISBN 978-1-118-29528-1 (EBK);
ISBN 978-1-118-29529-8 (EBK); ISBN 978-1-118-29530-4 (EBK)

PRINTED IN THE UNITED STATES OF AMERICA
10 9 8 7 6 5 4 3 2 1

THE ZEN of STEVE JOBS

SEPTEMBER, 1985, PALO ALTO, CALIFORNIA

...AND NOW WE TURN TO A BUSINESS NEWS UPDATE WITH RAY WHITE.

THANKS RIK. WE'RE GETTING WORD NOW THAT STEVE JOBS, THE CO-FOUNDER OF APPLE COMPUTER, HAS LEFT THE COMPANY AMID TANKING SALES.

NOT ENOUGH PEOPLE BOUGHT A MAC DURING THE HOLIDAY SEASON AND, AS YOU KNOW, THAT WAS JOBS' DIVISION OF THE COMPANY. INFIGHTING HAS BEEN RAMPANT SINCE.

INFIGHTING?

JOBS BROUGHT FORMER PEPSICO CEO JOHN SCULLEY ON TO RUN THE COMPANY IN 1983.

SCULLEY CURRIED FAVOR WITH THE BOARD FOR TWO YEARS. WHEN CONFLICT OVER SALES CAME TO A HEAD, THE BOARD SIDED WITH SCULLEY.

STEVE

ONE DAY, JOBS HAD 1500 EMPLOYEES WORKING UNDER HIM.

THEN HE HAD ZERO. SO HE LEFT.

SUMMER, 1986: TASSAJARA ZEN MOUNTAIN CENTER, CALIFORNIA

AFTER 11 HOURS OF MEDITATION.

STEVE! DOKUSAN!

SIT.

I RECOMMEND THE SEIZA POSITION.

YOUR LEGS LOOK LIKE THEY HAVE HAD ENOUGH FULL-LOTUS FOR ONE DAY.

MY LEGS ARE FINE, ROSHI.

HAS IT BEEN THAT LONG SINCE WE SAT TOGETHER? ABOUT A DECADE I SUPPOSE.

PLEASE CALL ME BY MY NAME.

I'M SORRY, KOBUN.

11

12

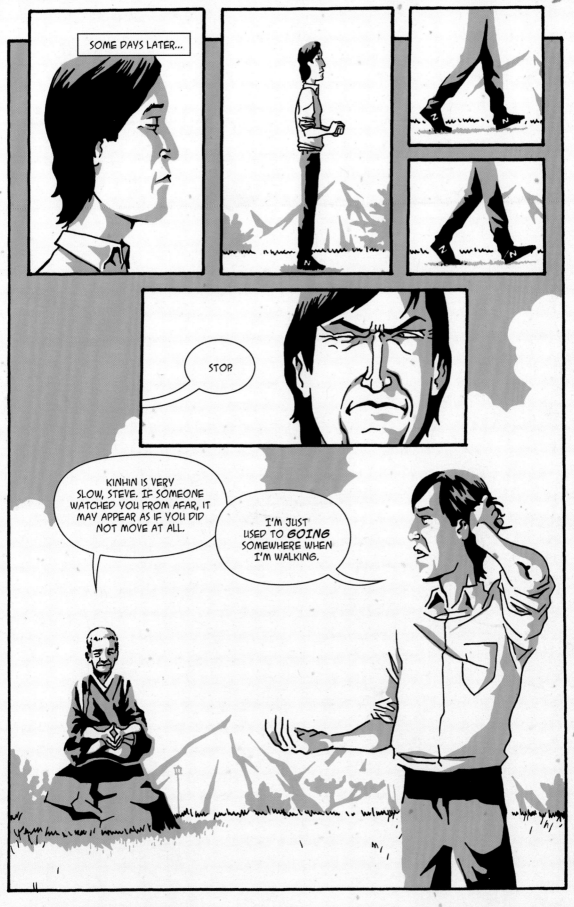

17

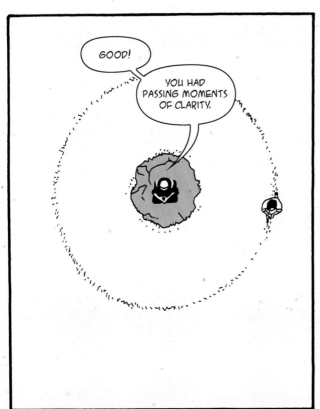

18

20

SUMMER, 1997: APPLE HQ, CUPERTINO, CALIFORNIA

HOW TO CHOOSE YOUR MAC

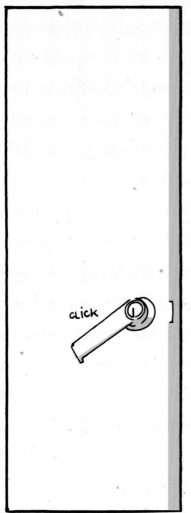

click

MORNING EVERYONE!

HOW ARE YOU?

LET'S CUT TO THE CHASE. YOU'VE ALL HEARD. AMELIO IS GONE AND THE BOARD HAS PUT ME IN CHARGE.

THE COMPANY IS IN DIRE STRAITS AND WE'RE RAPIDLY RUNNING OUT OF CASH. OUR PRODUCT LINE IS A MESS. WE NEED TO SIMPLIFY AND RE-CENTER. WE CANNOT AFFORD TO DO ANYTHING MORE THAN WHAT WE ARE BEST AT.

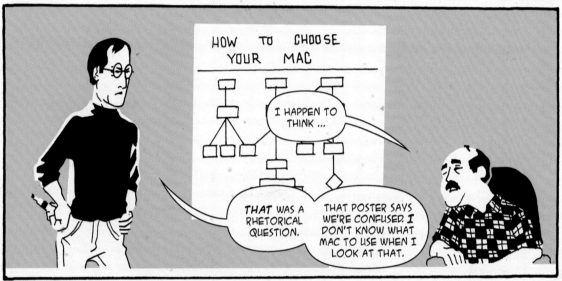

GOOD.

STEVE!

LOOK, WE'RE HAPPY YOU'RE BACK. BUT WHY ARE YOU KILLING OUR HARDWARE? WE BOUGHT UP NEXT FOR THE OS. THE COMPANY COULDN'T EVEN SELL ITS COMPUTERS.

NO.

WE COULDN'T.

SO HOW WILL THIS BE DIFFERENT?

SUMMER, 1986: THE JACKLING HOUSE, WOODSIDE, CALIFORNIA

THAT GARAGE WAS MY ZENDO. AND YOU SPEAK STRONG WORDS FOR A MAN WHOSE COMPANY ALSO STARTED IN A GARAGE.

BUDDHISM WAS NEW HERE. HE THOUGHT IT BEST TO ADHERE TO CUSTOM EXACTLY.

YOU DON'T.

ONE TEACHER CAN MAKE A VERY BIG DIFFERENCE.

SO WHY YOU?

MY FATHER, A ZEN PRIEST, HAD THREE SONS. HE TRAINED US ALL IN MEDITATION. I REMEMBER HIS HANDS ON MY BACK, CORRECTING MY POSTURE.

CANCER TOOK MY FATHER WHEN I WAS SEVEN.

AT FOURTEEN, I WAS ADOPTED BY HOZAN KOEI CHINO ROSHI. AS HIS ONLY HEIR, I WAS EXPECTED TO TAKE OVER HIS TEMPLE.

THEN UNIVERSITY. BUT IT DIDN'T FEEL URGENT ENOUGH. SO MUCH DEBATE, BUT NEVER ACTION. I LEFT FOR THE MONASTERY, WITH THE INTENTION OF STAYING FOR THREE DAYS.

I STAYED FOR TWO-AND-A-HALF YEARS.

THAT'S WHERE I MET THE KEISAKU.

UNIVERSITY TAUGHT ME TO ARGUE. BUT YOU CANNOT ARGUE WITH MONKS. THEY ARE ILLOGICAL. YOU SIMPLY HAD TO BE READY ON TIME. AND STRONG.

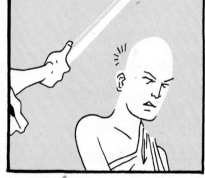

WHILE AT MONASTERY, I RECEIVED THE LETTER FROM SUZUKI ROSHI, ASKING ME TO COME TO CALIFORNIA.

I ASKED CHINO ROSHI FOR PERMISSION TO GO. HE SAID 'NO!' I ASKED A SECOND TIME, AGAIN HE SAID 'NO!' TRADITION SAYS ON THE THIRD 'NO' I MUST SUBMIT.

I DID NOT. I CAME HERE. CHINO ROSHI SAID "THAT LETTER IS A MAD DOG THAT WILL TAKE YOUR LIFE."

YOU DID WHAT YOU NEEDED TO DO.

WHAT I WANTED TO DO.

34

IT WAS WONDERFUL TO SIT WITH YOU ALL THIS MORNING. I AM PLEASED THAT KOBUN CHINO SENSEI WILL BE STAYING ON AS RESIDENT PRIEST. HE IS BOUND TO BRIGHTEN THE ZENDO.

AND NOW LET'S ENJOY THIS DELICIOUS FOOD!

YOUNG MAN, I DO NOT KNOW YOUR FACE.

I'M STEVE.

AND WHAT BRINGS YOU HERE?

UHH... AUDITING, I GUESS. CHECKING IT OUT.

YOU AREN'T ONE OF THOSE BEATNIKS, ARE YOU?

BECAUSE BUDDHISM IS MORE THAN FORTUNE COOKIE WISDOM. IT IS MORE THAN A RHYME TO BE EXHALED OVER THE BEAT OF DRUMS.

AND AMERICANS TEND TO OVER-INTELLECTUALIZE IT. AS SOON AS YOU INTELLECTUALIZE SOMETHING, IT IS NO LONGER WHAT YOU SAW.

I DIDN'T MEAN TO BE A BOTHER.

THE NEW PRIEST IS VERY DIFFERENT. HIS APPRECIATION FOR TRADITION IS... LOOSE.

PRIESTS ARE CHARGED WITH LIMITING THOSE WORLDLY OBJECTS THAT COULD PREOCCUPY US.

THERE ARE NO ENLIGHTENED PEOPLE. THERE IS ONLY ENLIGHTENED ACTIVITY.

THE NEW PRIEST BREAKS WITH TRADITION HE DOESN'T AGREE WITH?

NICE TO MEET YOU, ROSHI.

HI, I'M STEVE.

STEVE! IT'S A PLEASURE. ARE YOU FROM LOS ALTOS?

I GO TO HIGH SCHOOL IN CUPERTINO, ACTUALLY.

SUZUKI ROSHI TOLD ME A LOT ABOUT YOU. I THINK WE'RE GOING TO GET ALONG REAL WELL.

TASSAJARA ZEN CENTER, CALIFORNIA, 1986

WIELDING A WEAPON IS AN ART.

AND TODAY, I AM HERE TO SHOW YOU THE ART OF THE SWORD.

PRACTICE...

PRECISION...

SO, APPARENTLY, IS SHOWMANSHIP.

...AND RESTRAINT ARE KEY.

AND NOW KOBUN CHINO ROSHI WILL DEMONSTRATE WITH THE BOW.

THUNK

PERFECTION IS NOT EVERYTHING.

REDWOOD CITY, 1995

TOY STORY BLEW THEM AWAY! AND IT WAS ALL MADE ON COMPUTERS. IT WAS AMAZING!

YOU HAVEN'T MENTIONED PIXAR IN YEARS.

THEY'VE BEEN OPERATING IN THE RED EVER SINCE I BOUGHT THEM FROM LUCAS, BUT NOT ANYMORE!

I'M GOING TO START SHOWING UP AT THEIR OFFICES MORE OFTEN, I THINK.

WHICH MEANS I'LL START TRAVELING BY HELICOPTER.

HELICOPTER?

EVEN IN GOOD TRAFFIC, IT'S AN HOUR TO THE PIXAR OFFICES.

OH.

BUT ENOUGH ABOUT ME, HOW'S THE WIFE? STILL ON THE SECOND, I HOPE? OR DID YOU SCREW THIS ONE UP TOO?

KATRIN HAS BEEN GARDENING AND HATSUKO IS HEALTHY. EVERYBODY IS WELL. WE WANT TO HAVE ANOTHER, SO HATSUKO HAS SOMEONE TO PLAY WITH.

AND I'VE BEEN DOING A LOT OF TRAVELING, MYSELF.

YEAH?

I'M STARTING A NEW TEMPLE IN SWITZERLAND, AND I JUST CAME BACK –

HOLD ON A SECOND, KOBUN. I MISSED AN IMPORTANT CALL.

DIDN'T PICK UP. YOU WERE SAYING?

A NEW TEMPLE. IN SWITZERLAND. AND I JUST RETURNED FROM JAPAN

I MET CHINO ROSHI THERE.

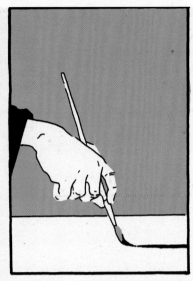

ME?

TRY THIS CHARACTER. COME, LET'S SEE SOME OF THIS FAMOUS CHOOTSPAH.

GESUNDHEIT. IT'S CHUTZPAH.

FUCK.

IT'S BEEN A WHILE SINCE COLLEGE.

IT IS A GOOD FIRST MISTAKE.

WHAT DO YOU SEE ON THE PAPER?

... YOU THINK THE DULCIMER SHOULD HAVE AN FM RADIO IN IT?

THE MORE WE WORK WITH THIS HARDWARE, THE SMALLER WE CAN MAKE IT. JUST THINK! SMALLEST MP3 PLAYER, LONGEST BATTERY LIFE, MOST SONGS, FASTEST UPLOAD AND RADIO TO BOOT!

WHY WOULD THEY WANT A RADIO? THEY HAVE ALL THEIR MUSIC WITH THEM.

TO BREAK DOWN THE TOP 40 WITH CASEY KASEM. TO LISTEN TO *THE SPLENDID TABLE.*

THAT'S A BOZO IDEA. IT'S NOT SOME SWISS ARMY KNIFE TO SHOVE TOOTHPICKS INTO.

KNOCK KNOCK

WHO IS IT?

GOT SOMETHING FROM SCHILLER.

I LIKE THIS – A LOT.

SCHILLER SAID SOMETHING ABOUT FLIPPING THROUGH SONGS FASTER, THE FASTER YOU TURN IT.

SEE THIS? SIMPLICITY. I WANT OUR CONSUMERS TO EXPERIENCE THAT. WHAT WE LEAVE OUT...

APPLE HQ, CUPERTINO, CALIFORNIA, 2000

RING RING
RING
RING

YEP.

A MAN TO SEE YOU. A KO-BOON.

KOBUN?

YES, THAT'S IT.

WELL SEND HIM IN!

KOBUN! IT'S BEEN SO LONG.

IT HAS. HOW ARE YOU?

FANTASTIC. BUSY, BUT GREAT.

OH. YEAH, PLEASE.

THE IMAC IS QUITE THE SUCCESS.

BEAUTIFUL, ISN'T IT?

IF EVER INDUSTRY COULD IMITATE ART.

IMITATE MY ASS. THIS *IS* ART.

IT HAS BEEN QUITE SOME TIME SINCE WE SAW YOU AT THE ZENDO.

LIKE I SAID, I'M *VERY* BUSY.

DO YOU FIND TIME TO SIT?

SOMETIMES. WHEN I FIND THE TIME.

I COULDN'T HELP NOTICING ON THE WAY IN THAT YOUR CAR IS PARKED IN THE HANDICAPPED SPOT.

NO ONE USES THAT. AND IT SAVES ME TIME.

I THINK THIS CHIP IS UGLY.

WHAT DOES IT MATTER? NO ONE WILL SEE IT.

CAN'T MAKE THE IMAC WITH AN ATTITUDE LIKE THAT.

PERHAPS YOU COULD MAKE A TRIP UP TO TASSAJARA SOON.

MAYBE.

I SHOULD GO. YOU'RE VERY BUSY.

GOOD TO SEE YOU, KOBUN.

STEVE, THE SIGNIFICANCE OF OUR LIVES IS NOT FOUND IN CREATING SOME PERFECT THING. APPLE, THE IMAC, THESE THINGS CANNOT DEFINE YOU.

TELL THE NEWSPAPERS THAT.

DO NOT LET APPLE BECOME YOUR MAD DOG.

58

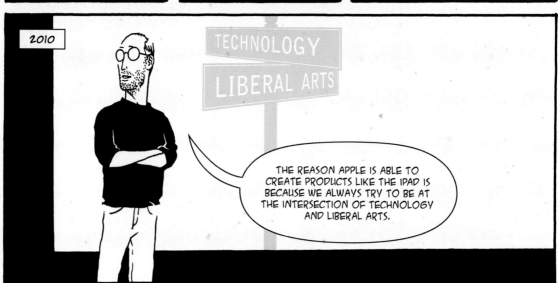

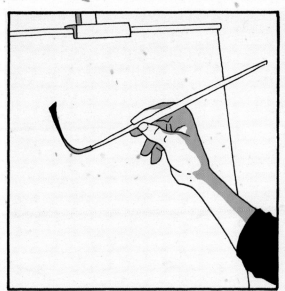

CALLIGRAPHY CAN TELL YOU A LOT ABOUT A PERSON.

IT IS NOT LIKE ANY OTHER ART.

IF YOU HESITATE, IT WILL SHOW ON PAPER.

THERE ARE NO SECOND TRIES.

DADDY!

AFTERWORD

Apple cofounder Steve Jobs had such an enormous impact on so many people and businesses that his life often took on the aspect of myth. Jobs encouraged others to think of him in this way, using his charisma and forcefulness to create what was called a "reality distortion field" that beguiled people to his point of view. But much of Jobs' impact and fame was due to collaborative work with designers, engineers and thinkers whose love of the spotlight was not as great as his. The *Zen of Steve Jobs* tells the story of Steve's relationship with one such person: Kobun Chino Otogawa.

Kobun was a Zen Buddhist priest who emigrated to the U.S. from Japan in 1967 and presided over temples in California. He was an innovator who lacked appreciation for rules. His move from Japan to California broke with tradition. So did his adamant rejection of corporal punishment. His students describe a priest who defied dogma constantly, preferring to tailor teachings and rituals to his individual students. Kobun was to Buddhism what Steve was to computers and business: a renegade and maverick. There is little wonder as to why the two became so close.

The story is extensively reported, largely through interviews with Buddhists who studied under Kobun and who sat in meditation along with Steve. The most useful sources knew both men and experienced their shared encounters. Many of Kobun's former students are now priests themselves. The unique philosophies and traditions of their temples reflect Kobun's devotion to customized educations.

From interviews with these Buddhist priests, I gleaned what Steve hoped to learn from Kobun as well as the nature of their public relationship. It quickly became apparent that Steve was most

devoted to religion when his life's path was at its rockiest. But what actually transpired between the two when they were alone cannot be known, at least not with the veracity of a traditional biography. That's why we call this book a "reimagining."

The story structure is non-linear, and mimics Steve and Kobun's relationship, which was stop-and-start, depending on Steve's changing life situation. The monochromatic palette, which JESS3 designed to change from scene to scene, also reflects this idea.

Kobun's role in Steve's life has not been fully explored in biographies, all of which have been content to simply mention that Kobun acted as a "spiritual guru" for Jobs' computer company NeXT, and that Kobun officiated the wedding of Steve and his wife Laurene Powell. *The Zen of Steve Jobs* tells a fuller story of their relationship. Yet, this book is not a biography. It excludes people and scenes that any biographer would deem essential: Steve's battle with John Sculley, his role at NeXT, the company's abysmal failure and his relationship with his family. What is left is an illustration of the relationship between two great minds, whose divergent value systems would ultimately send them along different paths.

Writing *The Zen of Steve Jobs* for Forbes has been a dream. Forbes' passion for telling the stories of great business people is unmatched, and Forbes remains dedicated to that mission in a time when economic and industry circumstances make it exceedingly difficult. This book would not be possible without the vision and expertise of Forbes managing editor Bruce Upbin, who trusted a wastrel intern with the job of writing it and who furthered its reportorial foundation and encouraged its creative potential.

-C.M.

ABOUT KOBUN

Kobun was born in 1938 in a small town in Japan to a family with a rich lineage of Soto Zen priests. His father, a priest himself, died when Kobun was a young child. He was ordained in his early teens and adopted by another priest, Hozan Koel Chino Roshi. Japanese tradition dictated that Kobun, as Chino Roshi's heir, would inherit the abbacy of the temple in the future. Kobun went on to receive Dharma transmission from Roshi in 1962, officially making him part of Chino Roshi's spiritual bloodline, and granting him the authority to teach and to transfer Dharma himself.

Kobun attended university in Kyoto from 1957 to 1965. During this time he trained in calligraphy and archery. After university, he spent three years at a Japanese monastery. He began training incoming students toward the end of this stay. In so doing, he broke with tradition by setting aside the Keisaku, a stick designated for corporal punishment and guidance in aggressively training young students. This marked the first of Kobun's many innovations in Soto Zen Buddhism.

IN 1967, while at monastery, Kobun received a letter from Shunryu Suzuki Roshi, who was teaching in San Francisco, and had been since 1958. The letter invited Kobun to come to California to help establish Tassajara, the first Zen monastery in America. Kobun's master disallowed him from leaving for America. Ignoring tradition yet again, Kobun disobeyed Chino Roshi and left for California anyway.

In the early 1970s, Kobun became the resident teacher at Haiku Zendo, located in suburban Los Altos. It was then that he first encountered a very young Steve Jobs. Haiku, named for the seventeen seats it housed, was merely a remodeled garage, illustrating Buddhism's humble beginnings in the States. The location quickly became too small for the large following Kobun gathered. During this time, Kobun married his first wife, Harriet. The couple had two children.

Kobun and Harriet divorced in the 1980s. Harriet moved with the children to Little Rock, Arkansas. For a period, Kobun moved to New Mexico, so he could be within driving distance of his family. Late in the 1980s he began visiting Europe to help former student Vanja Palmers, who was instructing Zen Buddhist students in Germany, Switzerland and Austria. Kobun helped Palmers and others establish new centers across Europe. While in Europe, Kobun met his future wife, Katrin. The couple went on to have three children. Kobun helped found numerous other centers, temples, monasteries and a university in the United States. Kobun and Katrin moved to Santa Cruz in the 1990s where they lived with their three children.

In Switzerland in 2002, Kobun drowned while attempting to save his five-year-old daughter Maya, who had fallen off a dock into a pond. Maya died as well. Kobun left behind a brilliant legacy of new Dharma heirs who continue to grow Buddhism in America and Europe.

A CONVERSATION WITH THE AUTHOR

Why did you choose to focus on this one period in Steve's life and his relationship with Kobun Chino Otogawa?

A full-length biography was out of the question. Jesse Thomas of JESS3 had talked with Forbes managing editor Bruce Upbin shortly before I arrived at Forbes in New York city, wanting to do a collaborative story that looked at the development of Steve's design aesthetic. That focus really got at the heart of both Steve and apple, without requiring a more comprehensive longitudinal narrative.

Steve, throughout his life, dabbled in numerous modes of Self-improvement and self-actualization. He experimented with drugs and, for a time, he only ate fruit, believing that doing so would keep him from sweating (talk about devotion to perfection). Zen Buddhism stuck with Steve the longest, and Kobun was Steve's mentor, in both Buddhism and design. The Buddhist priest was so influential in Steve's life during the mid-1980s that Steve named him NeXT's spiritual guru. But what really got me was the strong parallels in their worldviews — they are both rule-breakers and innovators. The idea of telling those stories in tandem really excited me.

What's the most interesting piece of information you found out during the research for this story?

The overarching narrative about perfection was, and still is, the most perplexing theme I encountered while researching this. I wanted to know what the "Buddhist" perspective on perfection was. Now, to talk about "Buddhism" is kind of like talking about "Christianity." There are numerous sects with their own schools of thought and particular traditions. I'd ask my sources: "what does Buddhism say about perfection?" They all laughed at me. I guess I'm kind of revealing my doctrinal catholic roots, but I expected a clear-cut answer. There wasn't one.

Steve believed in perfection. Kobun didn't. He believed in self-betterment, sure, but he also believed in achieving peace within oneself and with one's surroundings. Perfectionists are never at peace. In popular culture, we like to think of Buddhist priests as being these absolutely serene and wise individuals. But Kobun's life was filled with tumult. In the end, that's what drives these two men apart. One of them wants to be the perfect innovator making perfect products on a massive scale. The other is working to achieve peace with himself, his family and his surroundings. When Steve starts kicking ass again in the 90s, he and Kobun no longer see eye-to-eye. Perfection is the nail that drives that splinter.

What didn't make the cut that you really wish you could have found room for?

I drew inspiration from *Calvin and Hobbes* creator Bill Watterson when writing this. I wanted to focus on the relationship between Steve and Kobun, like Watterson did with *Calvin and Hobbes*, which meant actively excluding scenes that would introduce characters that would bog down the development of that relationship. So a lot of scenes didn't fit. Steve's wife Laurene Powell was incredibly important to him, and Kobun officiated the couple's marriage. But I couldn't introduce Laurene only to make her disappear. Their marriage is one of the best-documented public interactions between Steve and Kobun, but I had to let it go.

And finally, why tell this story through a graphic depiction rather than in words?

The written style of the book is kind of epigrammatic. It mirrors the style of the koan, a storytelling and learning device used largely by Rinzai Zen Buddhists (Kobun was a Soto Zen Buddhist himself). It's pithy. This style fits better with Steve's actual mode of conversation than it does Kobun's. Steve is a dramatic, direct speaker. Kobun was wise beyond measure but he was also something of a rambling lecturer. Had I not edited down those talks, they would have crowded the beautiful illustrations that JESS3 created. But there were wonderful kernels at the center of Kobun's lectures. So that was the point, to get to the essence of Steve and Kobun in such a way that the story could largely be told through images. In the end, this is an inherently visual story. The meditating, the calligraphy, the aging are all innately visual. It's also a book about design. You can write about design, or you can illustrate design. This is a story that was meant to be told graphically.

THE MAKING OF THE ZEN of STEVE JOBS

Check out the many faces of Steve Jobs.

"We have always wanted to do a technology —themed zine, with Steve Jobs as an obvious protagonist. Years ago, I caught an interview where Jobs talked about his time in Japan and how influential it was on the products that Apple makes. Fast forward to the spring of 2011: I was having lunch with Bruce Upbin, the managing editor of Forbes, so I went for it and pitched the idea. I said let's do a graphic book about Jobs' time in Japan, with an epic and reverent theme. Bruce loved it and we got to work. Halfway through production, Jobs passed away, which made the endeavor all the more important. This project is a dream come true." —Jesse Thomas, CEO and founder of JESS3

"It was interesting to see how Steve's progression of style and physical appearance correlated with his 'Think different' approach to life. From the simplicity of his blue Jeans, black shirts and the circular eyeglasses to his shaggy '90s look, the team and I did our best to capture his various styles in our renderings of Steve Jobs from the 1970s to 2011."
— Noah Smith, illustrator

SKETCHES
AND
STORY BOARDS

"The style is meant to loosely reflect the central element of calligraphy in the story. Heavy black lines and shadows clashed against suggested shapes and highlights are meant to mirror themes of Ma and spaces, hopefully in a way that represents the subtle atmosphere and introspection of the story."
— James Callahan, illustrator

"We went through so many different locks before we settled upon this final direction. Creating such a unique style was very rewarding. With the graphic book being about someone so high profile and familiar to us all, every aspect was fun to work on — especially as we started to see it all take shape."

— Chistian Day, global creative director

DESIGN IS NOT JUST WHAT IT LOOKS LIKE AND FEELS LIKE. DESIGN IS HOW IT WORKS.

COVER EXPLORATIONS

"The team and I felt the best route was to instill some of Steve's wisdom and ideology into the design and illustration of the cover. The inspiration was clean, simple, iconic. Ultimately, we decided to implement circles as the main design element, as they are so prevalent in many of the products that Steve introduced with Apple."
—Justin Harder, cover artist

Additional JESS3 team members who worked on this project behind the scenes:

Leslie Bradshaw   Becca Colbaugh
Jenny Redden   Simon Owens
Jehoaddan Kulakoff   Eric Leach

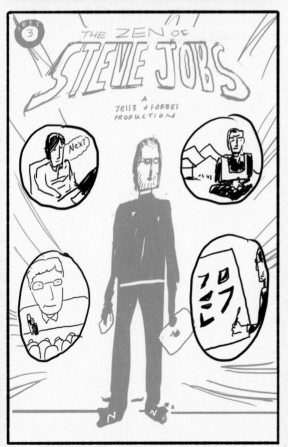

BILL GATES

For those of us lucky enough to work with Steve, it's been an insanely great honor. I will miss Steve immensely.

STEVE CASE

I feel honored to have known Steve Jobs. He was the most innovative entrepreneur of our generation. His legacy will live on for the ages.

PATTON OSWALT

RIP Steve Jobs. Closest thing we had to Tony Stark.

KATIE COURIC

Rest in Peace, Steve Jobs. You've changed forever the world you leave behind.

DICK COSTOLO

Once in a rare while, someone comes along who doesn't just raise the bar, they create an entirely new standard of measurement. #RIPSteveJobs

RANDI ZUCKERBERG

#SteveJobs was a pioneer who transformed the world and taught us to believe in ourselves. Thank you for inspiring us all, we will miss you.